BERKELEY TO THE BARNYARD

◦: A FAR CRY FROM HOME :◦

By H.E. STEWART

Helen Stewart

National Library of Canada Cataloguing in Publication

Stewart, H. E. (Helen Elizabeth), 1943-
    Berkeley to the barnyard : a far cry from home / H.E. Stewart.

ISBN 0-9693852-4-2

    1. Stewart, H.E. (Helen Elizabeth), 1943-. 2. Authors, Canadian
(English)—20th century—Biography. 3. Farm life—Rocky Mountains, Canadian.
I. Title.

PS8587.T4855Z464 2004   C813'.54   C2004-901181-2

PRINTED IN CANADA

Tudor House Press is committed to reducing the consumption of ancient forests.
This book is one step towards that goal. It is printed on acid-free paper
that is 100% ancient forest free, and has been processed chlorine free.

❧ DEDICATION ❧

In memory of E.B. White
for his wisdom and wit, his kind heart,
and especially his unique understanding of the barnyard

And for the dear friends and family
who have helped and encouraged me
in this work

ᨁ Turning Towards the Past ᨁ

I was young in 1965, the year we moved to the north. I was idealistic, naïve, and already married with a new baby daughter. My husband was ten years older, a graduate student of anthropology, and already well travelled in many lands. Now he wanted to try sheep farming. His special interest was in nomadic peoples, living with their animals in extreme environments. Perhaps this is why the far north appealed to him.

At the time, immigrating to Canada was not difficult, so with surprisingly little in the way of planning, we headed off, leaving behind friends and family, mild climate, and gentle California hills. When we reached the border of British Columbia, the customs officer greeted us cheerfully, glanced over our pickup truck loaded down with belongings, asked some questions, and then politely proclaimed us welcome to Canada.

This was a civilized beginning to be sure, but only a beginning, because we kept driving north, five hundred miles north on narrow roads turned to gravel, until we reached the small town of Jasper. To the west, the road nearly disappeared into the forest. Here and there along the way, planks had been put down over the mud. Randomly placed highway signs announced upcoming bumps, quietly under-stating what seemed a serious problem — for the entire way was hugely bumpy, strewn with stray boulders, great gaping holes, falling debris, and broken branches. Only irritating clouds of mosquitoes and swarms of biting black flies found this an easy path. We had truly chosen a road less travelled, and it did, indeed, make all the difference.

The road ended in a tiny town, surrounded by high mountains. I felt distinctly uneasy and somewhat sick at heart as we drove down the two blocks of dusty, empty main street. Old-fashioned board-walks lined small, shabby yards, a favoured few adorned with plastic

pink flamingoes. A handful of stores, mostly rather forlorn looking, had the feel of a movie set, a temporary backdrop for an old western. The only solid and pleasing structure was the railway station, positioned at the road's end, presumably the reason for the town's very existence. The railway, plus varied logging and farming operations, did in fact, provide most of the jobs.

For many valley people this was home and they seldom went away. For me, it was a far cry from home. I knew that people lived even farther north, much farther, but this was difficult to imagine.

The town was depressing to me rather than interesting, perhaps because I viewed the world as an artist, not as an anthropologist. I had studied music, painting and art history, and had rarely been away from my family's home in Berkeley. My father was a doctor and taught at the university. My young life had been well ordered and happy. It was also cultured, by comparison, and extremely sheltered, so I had no inkling of what lay ahead.

My husband began teaching French in the high school, a bonus to students who had never heard the language spoken properly. I tried to settle into the somewhat closed community, as winter settled into the valley. Days grew shorter, and the sun dropped behind the mountains, plunging the already dreary town into darkness, even before school let out for the day. Snow fell and the temperature plummeted. I felt as if we had moved to the North Pole, and would not have been surprised to see Santa appear in the midst of the whirling snowflakes. I would have asked him to carry me, with my child, magically away over these mountains iced with snow, back into the warm sunshine.

But that did not happen. We stayed on through the long winter and a short summer until the following fall, when my husband began teaching at the new university in Calgary, Alberta. Instead of settling in the city, we rented a house of three rooms, originally built as quarters for a dairy hand. This little box-like house was set on a huge expanse of farmland, even more bleak and cold than where we'd been before. A handsome woodstove dominated the kitchen, but there was no running water.

I found myself more isolated than ever, as is the way for count-
less numbers of farming women scattered across the prairies and the
northland. I had few outside chores because this was not our farm,
but I was far from the city and the university, and this was a different way of living, with a different sense of time and rhythm. I was
grateful for the CBC radio, linking this sparsely settled Canadian
country in its unique way, connecting me to information and a world
which seemed forever remote. Favourite radio personalities came to
be like friends in my empty landscape.

Two years later, following the birth of our second daughter, my
husband — always happiest when travelling — took a year's leave,
and we visited Japan. It was our return to the open flatness of the
prairies near Calgary which encouraged us to revisit the northern
country of our first migration. Having been immersed in the ancient
culture of Japan, we found the prairies bleak by comparison, so the
mountains and dark forests were a most welcome change of scene.

By chance we found a small and seemingly perfect sheep farm for
sale, a homestead situated on a southern slope, away from the town,
overlooking the wide river valley. With little thought to the logistics
involved, we bought this farm — house, barn, sheds, fields, and
pastureland, all clustered together on a cleared hillside, surrounded
by wilderness and high mountains. The house, with both electricity
and running water, was luxurious compared to other places we'd
stayed. It was cozy, covered in cedar shakes, with a back room of
sorts, a kitchen and main room, plus a real bathroom and two little
bedrooms upstairs. Best of all, I now had a wringer-washing machine,
even if it was down in the dark basement. My husband, who seemed
to relish hardships, especially as an observer, had finally realized that
washing clothes on a scrub board was not the best use of my time.

We stayed on this farm, off and on, for over fifteen years. We
adopted one baby boy, then a second, and lastly our third daughter
was born. My husband continued teaching far away, so I was often
left on my own to manage. I came to realize that anthropologists, like
writers, sometimes prefer observing from a certain distance. My husband was definitely a part-time participant, somewhat detached and

rather nomadic himself, continually on the move, collecting experiences along his way.

Though strange to me now, this was how we lived our life. Writing about this life has allowed me to gather together the thoughts and images in my memory. These images brought forth stories, and each story naturally had a way of calling forth another. So now, here they are, set down as they were remembered, more in rhythm with the seasons than in order of actual happening — my journey to the past.

⌁ THE BARNYARD ⌁

Morning came with the sound of hard rain hitting the window next to my bed. The rain poured down in the early darkness, thoroughly washing the sky and all the surrounding countryside, including our little farm.

I waited for a lull in this downpour, and then headed out to do the chores. Water dripped down from the eaves and from every small branch of the bare trees. Silvery drops fell quietly into dark puddles and into tiny streams trickling in crooked courses over the wet ground. The high mountains had disappeared behind gloomy, rain-dark clouds, and the barnyard, so shrouded in quiet mist, now seemed small enough to fit in the palm of one's hand. This was definitely a day designed to bring joy and happiness to ducks — but not to sheep. Patiently, the poor creatures huddled together, sad looking and sodden, surrounded by mud.

With my pail of grain, I ventured forth, holding my younger son, Toby, by the hand. Our rubber boots squished deep into the mud, and we had to concentrate on our steps in order to avoid being stuck. Suddenly, without warning, I was flung into the air and tossed sprawling, face down, splattering wet muck in every direction. Four-year-old Toby was left standing alone in wide-eyed wonder. My pail rolled away, spilling its grain, and my mind went spinning off in a muddle. I blinked the mud from my eyes and tried to spit the taste from my mouth. Whatever could have happened? I wondered.

Of course, it was the ram who had plowed into me from behind. I was afraid of him, and he knew it. Always he had the advantage. Warily, I lifted my head and looked about. Our faithful sheep dog was circling the scene, barking furiously at this terrible affront. The ram stood eyeing us with superiority, well pleased with the situation. He ignored the dog and prepared himself for another charge. I rolled out

of his way, struggled to my knees, and slowly stood, while Toby watched, quiet and bewildered.

All muddied and mucky, I sloshed back to the house, feeling sore and humiliated. Young Toby trailed behind, and then the dog, both of them solemn and obedient. When we reached the back door, the older children greeted us in dismay. Without a word, I headed for the bath, hoping for a bit of hot water. Toby quickly recovered and gleefully began to recount our adventure. I could hear his audience responding with frequent interruptions and giggles, then great gales of laughter.

For me, however, this was not a good beginning to the day. My back was black and blue, the chores were not yet done, and my boots were stuck somewhere out in the mud — probably by now collecting rainwater.

ॐ

This ram became especially protective during lambing season. Another time, and a different year, on a chilly morning out in the barnyard, I was bent over a ewe in distress, my hand up inside her, trying to untangle unborn twins. I was concentrating on the job, my young daughter beside me watching, serious and ready to help. I was fortunate to have children who helped. My oldest daughter, Katriana, was happy working with the animals, and my second daughter, Samara, loved baking and organizing the house, doing a better job than I could do myself.

Lambing was not easy, but there was no vet, and I could not always ask my good neighbours for help. I did the best I could, which was sometimes trying for the poor sheep. Now I searched about carefully for a small head, together with a pair of tiny forefeet, and then slowly eased them forward. After some tense moments, the first baby slipped out into the world, and as often happens, the second followed soon after without difficulty.

Baby lambs are soft and beautiful, with fine wool, clean and white. It was heartwarming to walk out into the barnyard and find a ewe with new babies beside her, on wobbly legs searching for their first drink. It was most disheartening to find a ewe in distress, and I always felt relief and gratitude when the babies were safely delivered.

The ram chose this moment of minor triumph to charge into me from behind, unfairly I thought, considering the circumstances. Once again he plowed into me, knocked me to the ground, and sent me sprawling. This time there was no mud, only frozen ground, so my landing was hard and uncomfortable, but not mucky. Once again I would be black and blue, once again stiff and sore, and worse, my peaceful musings were badly shaken as I was forcefully reminded of my tenuous grasp on farming life.

ॐ

After the lambs were born, I rubbed them down with a bit of hay and made sure they were able to drink. If there were triplets, the smallest sometimes had to be bottle fed. This baby, along with any other weak, sickly lamb, was kept in the house in a box near the wood-stove, cozy in a bed of clean straw. We could then watch over these little ones and provide frequent feedings, a rewarding job for the children, at least until bedtime. Then it was my turn.

Out in the barnyard, the other lambs grew stronger and ventured away from their mothers, running and leaping, frolicking together happily, gamboling about in the sunshine while the ewes looked on, undisturbed. When the inside babies grew strong enough, we put them outside with the others, but at our call, they would break off their play and come running to the gate for their bottle, delighting the children and any watching visitors. It was handy to have a few tame sheep, for it made handling the herd much easier. If one came running, all the others tended to follow.

So it is with sheep. They seem to think and act collectively. Individually, they sometimes appear a bit confused. The ram was an exception to this rule. There was never any doubt that he had a strong mind of his own.

ॐ

In the fall, I tried to keep this love-sick ram penned separately until breeding time. Of course, he had his own ideas, and was constantly escaping in search of greener pastures, dotted with woolly-white ewes.

One warm afternoon, as I was once again chasing him down the road, a flock of Mennonite children appeared in the distance, dream-like, in the shimmering sunlight. Surely, I thought, this must be divine intervention. Quietly and without fuss, the children spread across the path, forming a blockade. Effortlessly, they turned the ram around and encouraged him in a homeward direction.

"Perhaps we could lock him in the barn?" I enquired, my hopes rising as we galloped down the road behind the stampeding ram, who was, for the moment, uncharacteristically co-operative. Quite forgetting himself amidst the excitement and attention, he turned in at our gate and headed towards the barnyard. We followed on the run, instinctively circled around him, and slowly closed ranks. As if by prearranged plan, we joined hands and moved steadily towards the open barn door.

All at once, the ram became aware of our purpose and became agitated. He stopped, suddenly turned, and charged. Instantly, I leapt out of his way, breaking the circle and allowing his escape. The children, even the youngest, bravely held their ground and watched in concerned surprise.

Now we had to begin all over again. This time the ram was even closer to the barn door when he bolted. I jumped out of his way almost as nimbly as before, while the children, once again, remained serious and focused on the problem at hand. The oldest, kindest boy put forth an excellent suggestion — I should take charge of the barn door. When the ram entered, it would be my job to shut the door behind him.

This plan worked perfectly, and the ram was safely closed within the barn. He retaliated by ramming the door repeatedly with all his might. Miraculously, the door held. The children could now return home to tell their tale, and my lack of farming skills would once again provide a bit of entertainment for my hardworking neighbours.

I was left to devise a method for feeding this unpredictable animal, crashing about inside, continually clamouring to get out (providing insightful meaning to the words 'rambunctious' and 'rampaging'). Any one of my neighbours would have simply walked into the bam, shut the door and dumped out the feed, but I did not want to risk an escape, nor did I fancy being trampled.

Our barn was old, built of sturdy logs. It was not large, but was well proportioned, with a roomy loft above for storing hay. There was an opening in the floorboards, so the sweet-smelling hay could be tossed down to the waiting ram.

I could also easily climb the outside ladder with a pail of grain, and from the loft, pour the contents into the feed trough below. The water was a more difficult proposition. I rigged up a metal pail with a long rope tied to its handle, then climbed the ladder, and trying not to spill, pulled up my pail of water. Next, still trying not to spill, I lowered this pail to the waiting ram. He sometimes drank and sometimes rammed the pail, depending upon his mood, but because he was so grumpy, I allowed him only one chance.

I bumbled along with this tedious approach until the afternoon my neighbour drove into the farmyard, just as my water pail was poised midway up the ladder.

"Whatever are you doing?" he inquired politely. He tried to hold back his mirth, but could not help breaking into a smile. He must have considered my predicament further, however, because shortly after he drove away in his truck, one of his older boys appeared to help. Without hesitation, he constructed a strong wooden barricade, just inside the barn door, and in only a few minutes had solved my problem. I could now open the door, reach over the barricade and feed the ram without troubling to climb up and down the ladder. Why hadn't I thought of such a plan?

But then, I had never been introduced to a ram before moving onto the farm. I did not have the skills and ingenuity needed for this job, nor did I have my neighbours' astounding ability to deal calmly and sensibly with the ever-present mishaps and challenges of farm life.

✦ Bear Country ✦

In the beginning, nothing on our farm was familiar to me. I did not know how to care for the animals, and worse still, I was afraid of any large animal, including the ram. There were even larger wild animals living close by in the woods, and nearly all of them were interested in eating our sheep.

Soon after settling into our farmhouse, I walked down the dusty gravel road to meet my nearest neighbour. Looking up the driveway through the trees, I saw a big black bear, pawing at her screen door, and like a startled young rabbit, I stood gazing, totally transfixed. Before long, the neighbour came to her door, discovered this unexpected visitor, and began simply to shoo him away with her apron. I continued to stand and stare, still spellbound. Bears at the back door were far from my realm of experience. I had been a student living in a university town. Now here I stood, watching my neighbour calmly shoo away a big bear. Clearly, life as I knew it was changing.

Vast untouched and untamed country spread for miles in every direction. Long winters, deep in snowy darkness, were part of this landscape. Wild life was plentiful, including black and grizzly bears, as well as any nuisance bear from Jasper Park. The poor park bear would be tranquilized, then carried by helicopter in a big dangling furry brown bundle, and dropped at the park boundary, which happened to be the mountaintop directly above our farm. Upon waking, the bear would inevitably head down the mountainside, looking for the nearest garbage can, which happened also to be ours. These park bears could be troublesome, but the wild bears seldom bothered the sheep.

ʤ

Of course, if any bear was suddenly surprised or startled, or if any person mistakenly came between a mother bear and her cubs, the consequences could be terrible.

This is what happened on a hiking trail near Mount Robson one

of our last summers in the north. Our whole family had been camping near the base of the mountain, and in the morning had packed up and started down the long trail. We hiked all day. Our youngest daughter, Sarah, was perhaps six years old at the time. On the sunny way up, she had carried the marshmallows in her tiny plaid backpack. Now, even without this responsibility, she could hardly keep going. She was tired of hiking and tired of camping. She wanted to be home again, cozy in her own bed. Her older brothers and sisters (all carrying sizeable packs) took turns trying to encourage her.

It was growing late and the trail was steep. The great mountain loomed above, almost completely hidden in a gathering of huge heaping storm clouds. A faint, far-off rumbling sounded, and rain began to fall. As often happens in the Rockies, the first big drops quickly turned into a drenching downpour, and the trail into a flowing creek bed. Hiking wasn't fun anymore.

Crashing thunder rolled across a sinister sky, as early darkness descended. A flash of lightening revealed other campers rushing past, streaming down the mountainside, along with the torrents of rain. As in a dream, a Mountie appeared with an ominous warning: "Hurry down. A woman has been hurt. An angry bear is somewhere nearby."

No one felt tired anymore, not even Sarah. We were down the mountain in record time, all sopping wet, all soaked through and sodden. Excited and exhausted campers quickly piled into their vehicles with their wet gear, ending a desperate race down the mountain. One by one, we drove away into the dark and rainy night, grateful for the feeling of warmth and safety.

∽

An educational bumper sticker told the story: "Eat Canadian lamb — 10,000 coyotes can't be wrong." It was true. Deer, moose, and rabbit populations were all dwindling at the time, and coyotes were coming closer to the farms in search of food. Being extremely clever, they usually got what they were after, often causing great damage, and frequently killing without even feeding.

Coyotes are without scruples and without fear, attacking even in the daytime, usually aiming for a prize lamb. One registered ewe in the bunch, and a crafty coyote is sure to find it. Outwitting these cunning predators is difficult, perhaps impossible. We persisted in trying, although others before us had given up raising sheep in the valley.

Often we sent our two young boys into the fields to watch over the flock. Coyotes, to their credit, do not generally harm people. They are most often wary of even little people. So it was that Shepherd and Toby were out with the slow-grazing sheep on a sunny hillside below the house. As the sheep munched their way through the grass, the boys picked their way through a patch of wild sweet strawberries. I was working in the kitchen when suddenly I heard desperate cries. I ran to see what could be the matter and found Shepherd frantic, screaming and yelling as loud as possible. It was difficult to understand what had happened, but it seemed a bear had carried away Toby, our youngest child.

Now I was frantic, screaming and yelling as loud as possible. A story told in the valley came to my racing mind, the story of a bear carrying off a small baby from its basket, in sight of his horrified mother swimming nearby in the river. She yelled louder than possible, swam to shore faster than possible, and with shoeless feet chased the bear into the woods. There she found her baby, lying on the ground — unharmed. The bear, it seemed, had considered the baby abandoned, and had carried it away with great care. When he realized someone was coming for the baby, he laid it back down.

Now I too gave chase. I leapt like a deer over a barbed wire fence, in spite of being heavily pregnant, and ran down the hillside towards the woods, making as much noise as possible. Fortunately, this time my husband was close by and heard the ruckus. I looked up to see his truck coming along the road, Toby smiling happily from the passenger window.

I fell to the ground, all energy spent, realizing that the bear had made off with a lamb for his dinner. At the moment this did not seem at all important to me. Later I thought perhaps this was a sign that I was neither truly faithful nor truly devoted to my sheep; perhaps it was proof enough that our pioneering farm life was really not for me.

Still we stayed on the farm for many more years, and the pattern of problems persisted, as did the doubts occasionally rising like bubbles to the surface of my preoccupied mind. Over time a new highway was built through the valley, allowing travellers to rush across the countryside. Farming life, however, remained much the same and the surrounding landscape mostly untouched. The majestic rocky mountains stood patient and unchanging, while the small town of Jasper became crowded with tourists — swarms of people adversely affecting our bear problems. Defying common sense and ignoring posted warnings, these tourists naively continued to feed the bears, greatly increasing the numbers needing to be tranquilized and carried away in bulky furry bundles to be dropped above our farm.

ॐ

One morning a neighbour came by with two tiny brown cubs in the back of his pickup truck. He said he had shot the mother without realizing there were young. Now the babies huddled together like frightened teddy bears, with softness in their faces and sadness in their eyes. Immediately my son wanted to pet one. Instinctively, I thought it best to test this suggestion myself, and slowly extended my hand, anticipating the touch of the richly rumpled fur. In an instant, a little paw swiped at me, a forceful flash of sharp black claws. Quick reflexes saved my hand from serious injury, but the strength in that one small blow put me forever in awe and fear of any bear, great or small.

Still, the idea of sending these small wild creatures off to the confines of a zoo was unspeakably cruel. Until recent years, bears have roamed free, each with a territory of hundreds of acres, each following their own way and causing no harm.

ॐ

The Mount Robson incident was an isolated story of attack and injury, but occasionally another alarming tale travelled the valley grapevine.

One night a huge black bear ripped open a neighbour's screen door. Displaced from the park, hungry and frustrated, he was intent on getting inside, most probably drawn to the irresistible smell of delicious roasting meat. A flock of frightened children scurried upstairs in their nightclothes, as their brave young mother held onto the door with all her might. Their father hurried upstairs also and quickly shot the bear from an open window.

⁓

There were less disquieting stories too, hardly considered worth repeating. At our own back porch one fine morning, there was a small commotion, as my two young daughters tumbled through the door, pale and distraught.

"We saw a bear," they burst out breathlessly.

"And what did you do?" I inquired.

"We ran down the hill. We remembered to climb a tree, but it was too little."

I could picture them, running down the sunlit hillside, pigtails flying, stopping to assess a small sapling which would have bent down with their weight. The hillside was steep and open, and the rough grass good for grazing. The clearing, however, was edged with close, dark woods. The trees grew tightly together, with branches interwoven, climbing up the mountainside to wildflower meadows that fringed the towering peaks above. Wild animals had lived in these woods long before any clearing began, and the thick trees continued to provide safe hiding and secret cover for predators who watched and waited for a stray sheep to come their way.

Lost sheep were one thing, young girls another. Now, however, all was well and my girls were safely home. Who knows, the bear might have been young himself, and might have trundled off in a different direction, alarmed to see people coming too near his woods — even if they were little people.

⁓

Any humourous bear story was gleefully related throughout the valley. A nearby forest ranger told of finding a small dead bear in the woods, tucking him safely into his freezer for later study, and then going away with his family for his summer's holiday. A young neighbour boy, attentively checking the property, noticed a porch light burning and diligently turned it off, not realizing that this outside light indicated a properly functioning inside freezer — a practical precaution in an area of frequent power disruptions.

Unknown to anyone, the house began to fill with a most incredible stench, and by the time the family returned home, the stink was untenable. Without delay, the whole freezer, full to the decaying brim, had to be hauled away to the dump.

This problem naturally demanded immediate attention. And such problems were always cropping up, like chickweed after a spring rain, an inherent part of farm life in a remote area. This life was demanding. Every day was an adventure of sorts.

After years of continual mishaps and near disasters, swallowing up hours and days of time, I found it hard to have any sense of moving forward. Gradually, my expectations began to change. Getting through one day's work at a time was enough, and many days I felt happy just for not falling too far behind.

⌁ CHANGING SEASONS ⌁

We had recently taken up farming and my husband was far away teaching. I was on my own, feeling freshly hatched into a new world myself, when I discovered the sickly chicken in the henhouse. Naturally, I felt responsible for this small life, but did not know what to do, so once again called my neighbours for advice.

On previous occasions, an older boy had been sent to my rescue, but lately, the helpers had been younger. This time the knock on my door sounded curiously low down, a sign I did not at first fully comprehend. I was therefore startled to find a young child standing outside, waiting to help me. Feeling extremely foolish, I followed him to the barnyard and into the henhouse. He studied the chicken for a moment, then with certain conviction, pronounced her sick. Without hesitation, he picked up the poor bird by the legs, carried her outside, lifted her into the air, and swiftly swung her to the ground, smashing her head against a rock. He tossed the lifeless bird down indifferently in a heap, and went off home, satisfied the problem had been solved.

This was not the outcome I had anticipated. Somewhat meekly, I retreated into the house, now determined to learn something about farming. I did not want to call on my neighbours again soon, knowing the next time I might find a toddler at my door.

Many experiences and many years passed, and I did eventually learn more about farming. Early each spring, the children and I packed up, left Calgary, and returned to the farm in time to do the lambing. The weather was chilly and bleak, the snow sometimes still deep in cold shadows, but as the air grew softer and days longer, the frozen ground began to thaw. Slowly at first, but more quickly with each passing day, melting snow dripped from the trees and the eaves. Small snowy avalanches slid from the roof and branches, plopping down wetly onto the slushy ground below. Melt water collected in puddles and streams, overflowing and running off in crooked

courses, down the hillside towards the river below. The air was filled with a bubbling, watery sound, like the swallow's song to come, a constant musical murmuring of trickling water, percolating down into the damp, rich earth.

In the far north, the change from winter to spring is dramatic, exhilarating in a way unknown in milder locations. Strength of character and spirit are needed just to survive a northern winter. With falling snow and bitter cold all around, it is difficult to recall the touch of warm sun, and hard to believe that spring will ever return. The bear's hibernation, the bird's migration, and the flower's retreat deep into the earth all seem the only sensible recourse when the countryside lies buried deep in snowy whiteness.

So it is that when the darkness of the year is past, and the world is once again turning towards the sunlight, a great hope arises. In this rush of lush and lovely springtide, gladness fills the air. The earth awakens, and the whole world rejoices.

ॐ

Friends had stayed in our house over the winter months, while we were away in Calgary. But now the season was changing, and it was once again our turn to care for the farm.

The first morning after our return, our friend offered to help with the chores one last time. He made ready by donning coveralls, heavy boots and gloves, then a bee mask and hardhat.

"What are you doing?" I inquired.

"Going to collect the eggs," was his reply.

I said nothing, but wondered uneasily how the rooster could have become so ferocious.

The next morning, I headed for the hen house feeling a bit anxious. I opened the door with caution. The rooster flew straight at me, in a mean temper, wings beating angrily. Perhaps he was just protecting the hens, but his behavior was not acceptable. Wearing a bee mask and hardhat to collect eggs was not acceptable either. I could clearly imagine my neighbours happening by, finding me in that ridiculous garb, egg basket in hand. Whatever would be my excuse? Normally, collecting eggs was a chore for children.

This time I called our friend Mrs. Settler, who was knowledgeable about birds of all kinds and especially fond of chickens. She kindly agreed to visit our troublesome rooster. After tea, we all traipsed out to the hen house. I opened the door with care, ready for the attack. To our surprise, Mrs. Settler hurried inside and swooped up the offending bird, all the while praising and admiring his plumage. (He was a Barred Rock and quite handsome.)

We drove Mrs. Settler to her home across the valley, she in her Sunday hat and gloves, the rooster sitting serenely in a box on her lap, all of us awed by her magical powers. She was, after all, well over eighty years old. I was less than half her age, young and healthy, and afraid of a rooster. I was the one piece that did not fit into this particular patchwork puzzle, a piece somehow plunked down randomly in the wrong place.

I know I was not the first to feel this strangeness, but it is odd that I did not consider, even for a moment, that I might be able to change my predicament. Pioneer women before me had no choice. Faced with unbearable hardship and loneliness, they were forced to use all their strength and energy simply to survive. I was not a pioneer woman, and I did have some choice. I could see the necessity and rewards of hard work for sure, but also the dangers of too much physical labour. Depression and broken health were common enough in our valley. Finding the fine balance necessary for living a good life is never easy. Like others around me, I was too busy, too tired, or perhaps too young to give necessary and needed consideration to this important concept.

∿ BITS AND PIECES ∿

When the children and I first visited the Settler farm, we approached slowly, driving uncertainly down a dusty road, scattering colourful chickens in every direction. Nearing the farmhouse, I stopped the car carefully, trying to stay clear of the many unusual looking birds, all congregated together, clucking contentedly.

The goose arrived on the scene just as I gathered up our bouquet of flowers and freshly baked cake. He did not trust this intrusion, and immediately spread his large, strong wings to sound the alarm. I did not trust the goose, so headed towards the house with caution. More worried now, the goose threw himself into a great commotion, beating and flapping his wings, hissing insistently. More worried myself, I ran for the front porch, cheered on by the children, leaning excitedly from the car windows. The goose chased after me, defending his territory with every ounce of his energy. I leapt over the low gate with every ounce of my energy, which was not quite enough, for I tripped, falling from all grace and dignity, crashing down into a heap.

Very quietly, the front door opened, and there stood Mrs. Settler in her pretty patterned apron, calmly and curiously looking down at me, sprawled in the corner, but with the cake miraculously upright on its plate.

This was the beginning of a long and pleasant friendship.

The goose and I never did become friends. He continued fearlessly to carry out his guard duty, until many years later when Mr. Settler died, at home and well into his nineties. The faithful goose then gave up. He died only three days later, knowing his life's work had come to an end.

∿

The Settlers were among the first to homestead in the valley. They built and lived in a small shed, their first home, which later became a home for their chickens. As with other early pioneers, hardships were many, and the workload staggering.

This fine old couple now gardened and continued raising chick-

ens. To me, it seemed as if they could use some help, but actually, they managed very well on their own. Both were beyond their eightieth year.

One scorching summer's day, we set out together to cover the green house windows in an attempt to protect the tender plants from the burning hot sun. I searched an old shed for supplies, and found numerous bundles of old newspapers stacked high, plus an unbelievably huge ball of string — little bits tied together hundreds of times over long years, a truly staggering ongoing effort. The gigantic ball resembled a curious museum piece, or perhaps a playful bit of modern sculpture.

As I stood staring, one of my favourite childhood stories came to mind, a story about Homer Price and three enormous balls of string. Perhaps writer Robert McCloskey had also been searching an old shed, and had come across just such a treasure as this. The thought was enough to set one's imagination dancing with joy, the image certainly vivid enough for the beginnings of a good story.

I was considering the possibility when Mr. Settler appeared, wanting to know what was keeping me. Quickly I gathered up the necessary supplies, then climbed the ladder in the greenhouse and began stringing up newspaper to cover the glass panes. Mr. Settler stood by, leaning on his cane, watching my work with interest.

"Be careful, lady," he cautioned. "Don't waste any string."

This surprising piece of advice almost sent me tumbling from my perch on the ladder.

Later, I realized this advice was reasonable, for such thrift and resourcefulness had been woven into the fabric of pioneering life by necessity. Even today, most valley people are exceptionally frugal and self-sufficient.

Now, I wish I'd bought the ball of string. The many bits and pieces, tied together over the years, would have been a fitting remembrance of my life on the farm. Caste in bronze, sitting in my garden, uniquely winding its way from past to present, such a piece would have its own tale to tell.

✌ PRACTICAL MATTERS ✌

Our Mennonite neighbours, with little faith in public education, must have been amused to see that we, with our suspect university studies, were quite inept concerning any practical matters. Farming, as it turns out, has a great deal to do with practical matters, especially the matter of repair — fixing sagging gates and falling-down feeding pens, mending old sheds, broken down barn doors and worn-out latches, patching leaking roofs and bursting water pipes, rebuilding old fences, untangling barbed wire, and always tinkering with the ancient tractor and other antiquated equipment.

From the beginning, troubles seemed stitched into the pattern of our small-scale operation, while our Mennonite neighbours managed their large and complex farming life with relatively few complications. Ours was originally a homestead parcel of a sensible fifty acres, then bit-by-bit we added another three hundred acres, mostly steep hillsides of dense trees and tangled underbrush. Small hayfields and barns, plus some open pasture and an odd assortment of ever changing livestock completed this patchwork piece. We attempted to keep fifty sheep (not counting the lambs), three horses, a collection of mischievous and entertaining goats, different batches of hens and turkeys, and, at one time or another, a dozen cows, a bunch of rabbits, a couple of pigs, a handful of ducks, a variety of barn cats, plus great gatherings of bees.

The cows were eventually sold because they, like the ram, had a habit of escaping. When a cow wanted to get out, she simply leaned against a fence until it came down, thereby allowing all the other cows ample opportunity to stampede down the road together (likely the reason these particular cows had been sold to us in the first place, a bargain my husband could not resist). Our pig operation ended abruptly and sadly, and our experience with raising ducks was no more successful. The ducks paraded about in single file, following the

children whenever possible — a cheerful, friendly, bright-eyed little band, lined up in their feathery best, all clean and bright. They were the perfect little troop for training our young border collie, always agreeable and manageable in a way unknown to sheep. It was impossible to put an end to such enthusiasm for living. But a farm is not supposed to be a collection of pets, nor is it supposed to be a zoo, so one winter before leaving, we gave the ducks to a neighbour and we never saw them again.

Our beautiful border collie was most important of all, but she was considered a family member rather than a farm animal. She did her best to keep all the other animals in line, and without her, I probably would have given up our farming venture early on.

~ A TRUE FRIEND ~

Border collies are made for working. One dog takes the place of many hired hands, without fail devoting its full attention and a joyful spirit to the task at hand. I needed my dog and relied on her help. She not only looked after the sheep, but sometimes the children as well, and because I was often alone, she became especially attentive and protective. The one time a strange, ragged looking man came to the door late in the night, she flung herself at him in a fury, barking wildly until he retreated to his battered truck and fled.

During lambing season, she followed me to the barn, usually twice during the long, frozen nights. The yard light provided some protection, but in the beginning, I imagined bears lurking every-where and depended on my dog to alert me to any nearby danger. Eventually, I did not worry about bears, but liked to have my dog with me just for her good company.

Inside, the barn was safe. It was warm and peaceful, with the sweetness of fresh hay and the wonder of new life. The ewes were penned separately with their babies and a heat lamp to give them extra warmth. There were only about six makeshift pens, so I had to constantly move around these little family groups, sometimes putting mothers and their new babies outside after just a day or two, in order to make room for another birth. If a lamb was born outside, it could quickly freeze to death.

One early morning, I found a pet sheep standing over her frozen baby, crying as if her heart would break. She stayed grieving in that place for two days and nights, until there was an extra lamb to wean onto her. Woolly, as she was called, was the best mother to any baby. Sheep, surprisingly, are like humans in this regard — some are excel-lent mothers and some do not care for their offspring.

Only after I had gained some understanding of my situation and some confidence in handling these matters, did I begin to appreciate

lambing time. There was an air of expectation and a feeling of Christmas Eve about the place, especially because the barn was set apart in the silent and snowy night, surrounded by infinite darkness.

ᴗ

There were other rewards for going out repeatedly into the night. Sometimes the northern lights danced across the sky, their magical and mysterious ribbons of colour lighting a darkness crackling with cold. My first encounter with this unusual phenomenon was disquieting, for I found the entire sky pulsating with bright colours, leaping like flames to the center of the vaulted universe. Naïve and alone, in my ignorance I thought perhaps the world was coming to an end.

Later, an older friend reassured me, and told me to also watch at night for a snowbow, a rainbow lit by the moon, shining through a mist of tiny, icy crystals, turning the cold and snowy landscape into a fairytale world of enchantment. She said the sight was worth her many years with an outhouse in place of indoor plumbing.

My night time trips to the barn were limited to a few weeks during lambing season, so I was never blessed with this magical vision, but it was encouragement enough just to consider the possibility.

ᴗ

When at last the snows melted, the sheep moved away from the barn during the day and into the pasture for feeding. Every evening at dusk, one or more of the family went out to the fields to gather them back in. Always, our dog led the way, eagerly anticipating the job to be done. She waited anxiously for permission, then raced away up the hillside with lightening speed and amazing grace. As the sheep munched their way across the rough ground, she worked her way around them, circling back and forth, gathering the group together, coaxing them along with care down towards the open gate. She crept close to the ground, only her head appearing above the long grass, ears alert, like a beautiful white fox. At some point, one of the sheep would break into a run and the rest would follow, flocking together, bells ringing, spilling down the hill and through the gate like a thick woolly cloud. I never tired of watching this sight, and each time was moved by the beauty of the scene.

Every night the sheep gathered into the fold close to the barn, a barn too small to hold them all. Only the outside yard light kept watch, warning predators to stay at a safe distance. Even an unusually bold coyote would not enter its circle of light, but if a foolish sheep strayed away into the darkness, even a more cautious coyote might be waiting. I wondered that a wolf was chosen for the story of Little Red Riding Hood. To my mind, it should have been a coyote.

Early each morning we returned to the barnyard, our dog alert and again glad to be at work. This time the sheep followed us across the field without encouragement. We simply opened the gate and watched them spill back into the upper pasture, ready to begin their day of grazing.

The repetition of farm chores gives a satisfying rhythm and routine to the day, and for me, the best part of this routine was having my dog always by my side. She was a true and trusted friend, loyal to the end of her long life. I often remember her and sometimes still dream of her. I will always miss her.

As for the rest, on our farm the disruptions were almost as regular as the chores, and the rhythm tended to be more erratic than peaceful.

⠒

Each morning after letting out the sheep, I continued on, with my dog at my heels, to do the milking. To reach the goat barn, I had to cross the horse pasture, bothersome only because I was afraid of the horse. I don't know why I felt so uncomfortable, perhaps because he was bigger than I and a bit wild. Luckily, his field of rough, grassy land covered many acres, and he was most often somewhere among the trees.

Milk pail in hand, I made a dash for the barn and quickly shut the door behind me.

Once safely inside, I relaxed into the peaceful ritual of milking. The barn was always warm and smelled of sweet hay. The two nanny goats stood contently in turn on their old wooden stand, calmly eating grain as I milked. At least one friendly barn cat regularly appeared, hoping for a drink of fresh milk, and the baby goats leapt about me playfully on tiny black hooves like little ballet dancers. Their joy was infectious.

After the milking, I always looked through a knothole in the weather-worn door to see where the horse might be. Usually he was nowhere in sight, so I propped the door open for the goats, and made another quick dash across the barnyard with my milk pail now full.

One day I put my eye to the knothole as usual and found a huge dark eyeball looking back at me. The horse and I, who never did see eye to eye, stood staring straight at one another in amazement. If W.C. Fields was correct when he proclaimed that anyone who hadn't seen themselves as a cartoon was missing the truth of life, then this was clearly an opportunity to discover a great truth. And I was being given time to ponder the matter as I waited for the horse to wander off.

Smug and self-satisfied, he was in no hurry to leave his prized position. I thought perhaps one of the children would come looking for me, but this did not happen. I called out my predicament, but still no one came. Finally, I had no choice but to feign indifference, sit down on a bail of hay, and quietly wait, hoping the horse would soon become bored and leave.

Outside, at a safe distance, my dog also sat down patiently to wait, no doubt wondering at this strange change in routine. Milking was supposed to be a calming and restful task, requiring but a few minutes, a chore which patterned the day with its own rhythm and natural order. This day the chore took up half the morning, until at last the horse went away.

꙳

My clothesline also had to cross over the horse's pasture. One end of the line was connected to a covered porch, for rainy day washing, and the other to a birch tree some distance away. The horse was usually far off in his field, but if he did happen to appear, he would occasionally come over to watch me hang out the clothes. His habit was to wait politely for me to finish the job, and then on cue, like a trained circus entertainer, calmly walk along the line, biting the tops of the clothespins, springing them open one by one, dropping the clean clothes to the ground below. He seemed to enjoy this sport most fully when the ground was wet and muddied.

I had to call my young son Toby to gather up the fallen clothes. From the beginning, he was naturally comfortable with animals of every size and kind. The horse never troubled him as it did me. If the clothes were mud spattered, I put them back into the washtub, through the ringer into the rinse water, then again through the ringer into my waiting basket. By this time, the horse was usually far away, so I could try once again to make use of the clothesline.

Because there was endless work to do, it was maddening for a simple task to gobble up so much time. The solution to the problem was obvious — merely move the horse to a different pasture. But simple solutions for us invariably had a way of becoming complicated. Moving the horse involved fixing miles of fence, building a corral and a covered shed for storing hay, and then coaxing the horse down the road to his new home. Each of these jobs required my husband's attention, and often he was not there. Nor could he understand anyone being afraid of a horse, so to him the problem did not seem urgent. It was frustrating only to me, frustrating enough to make me wonder once again just what I was doing in a place where washing clothes could possibly take most of the day, and where a horse could roam about quite freely, while I sometimes felt as if I was reaching the end of my tether.

⌁ DEEP IN PEA PODS ⌁

Our garden grew bigger every year, soon achieving monumental proportions. Even our farming neighbours with their prodigious number of offspring did not have such a garden.

Whatever could we have been thinking? Perhaps we were simply overly enthusiastic; perhaps too pessimistic, imagining row after long row necessary to grow the needed number of vegetables. Whatever the reason, we plowed ahead, and then had to spend the entire summer weeding and harvesting.

The combination of deeply rich soil, long days and frequent, refreshing rains made for lush growing gardens and quickly sprouting weeds. Like Jack and his miraculous beanstalk, we could see our beans growing bigger each day. Then suddenly, almost all at once, almost all the peas ripened. We picked bucket after bucketful, spilling out the delicious garden green, heaping our big kitchen table deep in pea pods. The children helped shell until past their bedtime, and I continued late into the night, with miles still to go and piles to shell.

The following morning, a visiting neighbour suggested an easier way of doing this job. Pleased to try a more imaginative approach, we gathered up the remaining harvest and paraded off to the laundry room, the start of another small farm drama. The children were in charge of props, and held their clean white sheets up high around the washing machine. As first performer, I began pushing the pods, one at a time, through the wringer, then ducking out of the way as the peas came shooting back at me, some bouncing off the walls and ceiling like hailstones gone astray.

The children found this immensely entertaining, watching from behind their safe cover of crinkly sheeting. A few peas did hit the waiting sheets, and a few did roll down to collect together in little piles, but the whole production was rather disappointing, not at all

what I'd imagined. The wringer, happily doing its part, squished each and every tender, young pea.

I quickly decided the old-fashioned way of shelling was most efficient after all, so the show ended, and we headed back to the kitchen with our pails, and once again began breaking open the fat pods. I did wonder if my neighbour was teasing with this suggestion, but recently, a retired farmer told me his mother had used this very method successfully. She, however, had blanched the pods before putting them through the wringer, an essential step not included in our instructions. But perhaps this suggestion too was made in jest, for softened peas would surely be squashed by the wringer.

⁓

My neighbours themselves occasionally tried out some original, timesaving plan. Our Mennonite neighbours once even attempted using their wringer washing machine for making butter. It did seem a good idea — to pour in the cream, turn on the agitator, watch the sweet yellow butter take shape, and then simply siphon off the buttermilk through the connecting hose. An altogether clever and sensible idea — except that it did not work. Gallons of rich cream sloshed about in the machine, as everyone watched expectantly, children flushed with excitement, adults somewhat more cautious, and me, enjoying myself in the unusual role of observer.

Nothing happened. Perhaps the cream was too fresh or too warm, but it did not turn to butter.

The next idea was to scoop out this frothy, messy mix for cooling in the freezer.

After a time, the cream was once again set churning, and once again, with hopes high, everyone, including me, gathered around to watch. Alas, once again, nothing happened. No butter. And by now, the washing machine and associated paraphernalia were completely gummed up with greasy cream. In a neat and tidy Mennonite household, this was definitely a sad state of affairs, a most embarrassing situation, made immeasurably worse by my presence.

In our household we had different standards. For us, the pageant of peas was entertaining and certainly not the slightest bit embarrassing. Problems, great and small, were plentiful on our farm, and a certain disorder was an expected part of our everyday life. I was becoming accustomed to this life, and by now had learned to laugh at my mishaps, knowing that otherwise I could easily despair. Plans and projects often seemed to be falling down around me, so a few peas hailing down on my head mattered not at all.

♫

The pea plant, with laddered structure and curling tendrils, is architecturally beautiful. Vines reach upward, petals fall, and blossom ends turn to pods, holding next year's seed. The little peas nestle all in a row in their tiny cradle, wrapped in their insulating blanket, moist and spongy green, its strong waxy lining protecting against sun, rain, and chewing insects — without question, the most perfect seed packet ever designed by the Great Designer.

I liked tending the plants, and did not mind the picking, but we all quickly tired of shelling. This endless repetition could be a meditation of sorts; for me, however, it turned to a tedious and time-consuming chore. After so many years of shelling buckets- and basketsful, I now plant just a few peas, for the continued pleasure of watching them grow and the certain satisfaction of eating them fresh. Added to these is the great luxury of sitting in my garden, drawing the vines, and feeling a special connection with this one small piece of our living, growing world.

↵ FALLING SKY ∿

Early on a summer's morning, quiet lay over the fields and fresh grasses, all wet with dew. The sheep stood hushed and silent, bunched together in the barnyard, peaceful and patient, waiting for the day to begin. Delicate drifts of mist rose from the river below, rearranged themselves and trailed slowly across the sleeping valley, still in the shadow of darkness. As the first pale light lit the mountain peaks, a rose-coloured glow spread into the sky and down over the mountaintops, like a delicate watercolour wash, announcing the dawn of a new day. The whole scene was reminiscent of a magnificent Chinese landscape painting, touched by magic. Such a sight was to be savoured, for sure. One knew from experience that this enchanted spell could be broken in a moment.

And broken it was, when a frightened goat named Snowflake decided this perfect world was coming to an end, that surely the sky was falling. With her head stuck inside a large peanut butter tin, she frantically charged about the field, bleating pathetically, the sound reverberating into this tin usually reserved for measuring grain. The clamour frightened her even more, and she echoed her alarm loudly across the land. My boys, as might be expected, felt no sympathy for the goat's complaint and nearly collapsed with laughter, thereby adding more confusion and merriment to this once dreamlike morning.

At all times, our goats could be counted on to provide entertainment. Compelled by curiosity and aided by outstanding agility, they carried on a continual investigation of new territory. The kids were especially endearing and mischievous, often slipping through the gate and suddenly appearing in the kitchen, once — inexplicably — on the hood of the car. One especially quick and nimble baby made a brave attempt to climb the biggest woodpile, setting the logs to rolling as he went, bleating louder and scrambling faster with every

step on his fast moving stairway, causing an avalanche of logs to tumble down around him, until he at last ended in a confused heap, crying in pathetic desperation.

There were, of course, practical reasons for keeping goats, for the nannies provided the extra milk used for bottle-feeding orphan lambs. Sometimes a new lamb could even be weaned directly onto a mother goat, and she would oblige, compatibly caring for the baby as if it were her own.

Goats are quick and intelligent, and therefore unlikely to be caught by coyotes. Ours wore bells around their necks and were put out to pasture with the sheep. If frightened, they would dash away in a bell-clanging panic, usually in the direction of the barn, perhaps encouraging the all too complacent sheep to do the same.

Unlike many other barnyard animals, goats are clean and fastidious; they would refuse to eat even slightly mouldy hay and would not accept a delicious fresh carrot from someone viewed with suspicion. Mostly I remember our little flock fondly because they added a light-hearted spirit to the barnyard and the farm. To our struggling operation, this was a highly valued contribution.

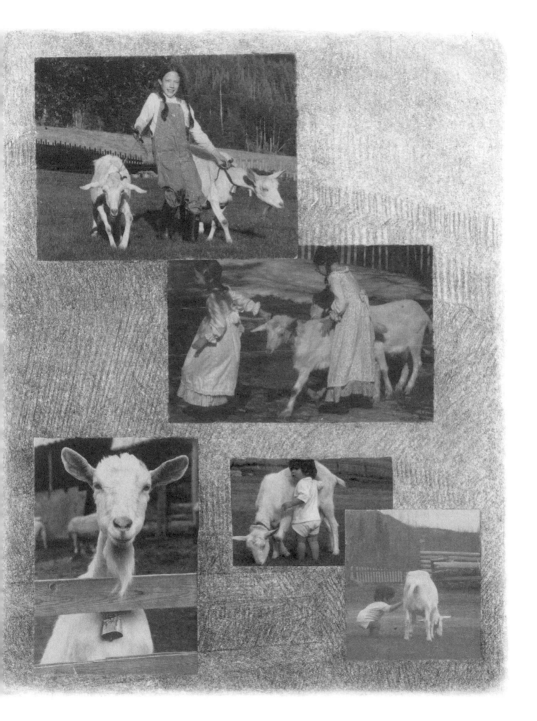

Picking blueberries was a favourite summer's occupation. It was a day away from farm work and an outing with good friends. It was a restful time apart, for the berries grew in a distant valley, tucked between high mountains, iced and snowy. A quiet stream meandered through the open valley, and on either side, steep rock walls rose to a great height. Waterfalls in abundance, fed by unseen glaciers, tumbled and trickled in delicate patterns down the massive rock faces. This was a majestic and magical landscape, a country where hobbits and elves might feel at home.

The valley was silvery blue with berries, so many that one could fill a pail, delicious to the brim, in no time at all, and because we had not tended to their growing, the gift seemed all the greater. The blueberries grew on low bushes, in clusters, like bunches of tiny, sweet grapes — perfect picking, especially for young children. Our huckleberry hunts, by contrast, always involved clambering over fallen trees and searching through dense forests, often wet with rain. Here the picking was easy. Many pails were full by the day's end, as were the pickers, their smiles and fingers stained blue.

Bears also gathered in this valley of plenty, stripping the blueberries with their large and surprisingly nimble paws. Even big bears ate almost daintily, at times happily licking and nibbling the berries from cupped, furry paws, like children with handfuls of tasty sweets. We wore bells around our necks to announce our whereabouts, but with such great abundance, there was no need for fear. There were blueberries aplenty, more than enough for all.

◡

Back at home the following morning, we began cleaning our berries. Ten pailsful was quite a task, for many of the pails contained a generous sprinkling of leaves, and many berries were still attached to tiny, wiry stems. (Cultivated berries are larger, easily plucked from

their stems, but lacking sweetness.) Following the advice of an experienced neighbour, I dumped all the berries into a bath filled with cold water. The berries were supposed to sink, as the leaves and debris floated to the top. A few leaves did indeed surface, but mostly everything just stuck to the wet berries.

The next suggestion was to roll the berries on a clean woolen blanket in order to separate them from the leaves. Out to the lawn we went, with our red Hudson's Bay blanket and our buckets of wet berries. Alas, this trick did not work either, but did stain the blanket blue with the juice of squished berries.

The final suggestion was to simply blow away the leaves with a fan. We plugged an old hairdryer into many lengths of extension cord, and blew away a few leaves. Meanwhile the day was passing, and we had made little progress in spite of our efforts. I had no choice but to sit down and pick the berries, one by one, from their stems. Hour after hour I worked, the children sometimes taking a turn. This was not a difficult task, but exceptionally tedious, taking time away from other work needing to be done. Other work always needed to be done. This was the nature of farming in the north. You did your best, but fell behind anyway.

Three days later, the berries were finished at last, although still appearing in my dreams. Fifty quarts were frozen, ready for coffee cakes and cobblers, pies and pancakes, muffins and jam. Like a squirrel with stashes of tucked away nuts, I felt more prepared for winter, although for the moment did not care to eat even one more blueberry.

⌇

After endless ages, the gently flowing stream and the beautiful valley of blueberries are now gone. In their place stands a backup reservoir for a large dam, its flood waters dirty, clogged with ancient uprooted trees, unsafe for boating of any kind.

As caretakers, we failed our pristine and magical valley. Even the bears must weep.

∿ A RESTFUL DAY ∿

I was at home with only my son Shepherd the day the house caught fire. I had finished tidying the kitchen, put some odd bits of paper to burn in the woodstove, and was starting to wash windows when the first whiff of smoke drifted into the stillness of the day. I was vaguely aware that this smoke did not smell like burning paper.

"Do you think the house is on fire?" I asked my three-year-old son, light-heartedly.

We proceeded outside to see what was happening. Standing together on the grass, we looked up at the roof, and sure enough, it was burning. Small flames leapt from the chimney and danced merrily across the wooden shakes. Instantly, I jumped into action, rushed to the laundry room, put a pail under the tap to fill, and then quickly went to put Shepherd into the bathtub, where I hoped he would be happy and safe, with a little water and a toy boat for company.

Next I hurried back for my pail and exchanged it for an empty one. The flow of water, fed only by gravity, was frustratingly slow, but I had no time to watch or fret. I grabbed my pail, and trying not to spill, ran up the stairs, through the bedroom, out onto the balcony, climbed over the railing, and then jumped across to the old roof. This ridiculous approach was the only possibility without a ladder, and I had no idea where the ladder might be, and no time for a search. I dashed through the house, with my mind racing along at a brisk pace, methodically sorting through each imagined room, deciding what should be saved.

I threw my water onto the fire, but nothing happened. Another dash for another pail of water. Another run up the stairs and another jump to the burning roof. Not until the third pail did the flames show any signs of receding. After many more effort-filled pails, the fire was reduced to smoking and smoldering. Only then could I take

time to rig up a hose, using a rake to reach it to the rooftop. Exhausted now, I sat astride the roof's peak with my trickling hose, soaking the scorched shakes as best I could.

An empty, black hole surrounding the chimney suggested the chimney itself had caught fire. (Of course there was no chimney sweep in the valley, and chimney fires were a common occurrence. A person was supposed to periodically climb onto the roof, drop heavy chains down the chimney, and rattle them about to loosen the buildup of soot, a chore we foolishly had neglected.) A spark must have fallen from this fire onto the roof, igniting a sprinkling of tinder dry moss, then flaming out like lightening, singeing all the shakes in its pathway.

My son, naked and shivering with cold, came outside looking for me. "Can I get out of the bath yet?" he called up to me, his teeth chattering.

All of a sudden, I was afraid — afraid of the fire, afraid of the height, afraid to get down, afraid of falling, and afraid of jumping to the ground below. The idea of leaping back to the balcony was inconceivable. Surely, I thought, someone will drive by and notice me on the rooftop, come to see what is happening, and bring me a ladder. I waited, but no one came.

It was beginning to grow dark, and my son had been cold for too long. I was forced to gather my depleted courage, slide down the slippery, wet roof, and drop from the eaves to the porch below.

Shepherd watched this unfolding drama with anxious interest. Just as I completed my tricky leap to the ground, our car turned into the driveway, and the rest of the family returned home from their day's outing. They found me smudged with soot and dripping wet. Shepherd was blue with cold, his teeth still chattering. When I explained what had happened, my husband was only disappointed he had not been the one to put out the fire — an experience, he said, he had always wanted to have.

I said nothing, but was more than disappointed he had not been the one on the rooftop. Fit and energetic, he never was satisfied with ordinary life. Always seeking adventure, he loved climbing mountains. I am afraid of heights, and had stayed home, feeling neither energetic nor adventurous. Secretly I had wished for one summer day of restful quiet. I longed for a bit of time to read or draw.

My young life had been an endless string of carefree days, which at the time seemed not at all unusual. Now I could hardly imagine such luxury. I could no longer imagine even one such restful day.

∽ BETRAYAL ∾

We went to visit a batch of baby pigs at our friends' farm. I felt well acquainted with pigs, having just read *Charlotte's Web* to my children (and then again to myself, for its reassuring and optimistic look at farm life).

Like Wilbur, the babies were adorable, and we came away with two, tiny and pale pink, snuggled together in a box with some hay. A single piglet, I thought, might suffer from loneliness.

We had a good place for pigs — an old log barn on the hillside across the road from our farmhouse. Trees had grown up around this barnyard, providing dappled shade to the clearing; an overgrown pathway led to a tumbling-down cabin and a big, open field, steeped in sunshine. Once the hay had been brought in, the pigs would be able to root around here to their hearts' content. With plenty of grain, extra goat's milk, and leftover scraps, the situation seemed ideal.

The pigs were very sweet. They were clean, intelligent, and extremely friendly. Whenever I arrived with a pail of food, they ran to greet me with squeals of delight and a grand show of enthusiasm. Too soon, however, these darling little piglets turned into bigger pigs, and as summer passed, they continued growing, until they stood waist high and huge. Like a new mother, who can not imagine her baby as a teenager, I had not imagined our pigs fully grown, and was not prepared for this sequence of events. Now when I arrived with my pail, the pigs came trumpeting up the hillside like elephants, and I was afraid of being flattened by their exuberance or trampled in their mealtime excitement.

I felt compelled to change my approach, and began quietly sneaking up to the barn at feeding time. Then one day, in the afternoon stillness, I heard an incredible loud bellowing, like the sound of a trapped or frightened wild animal. But no, it was only a pig, only

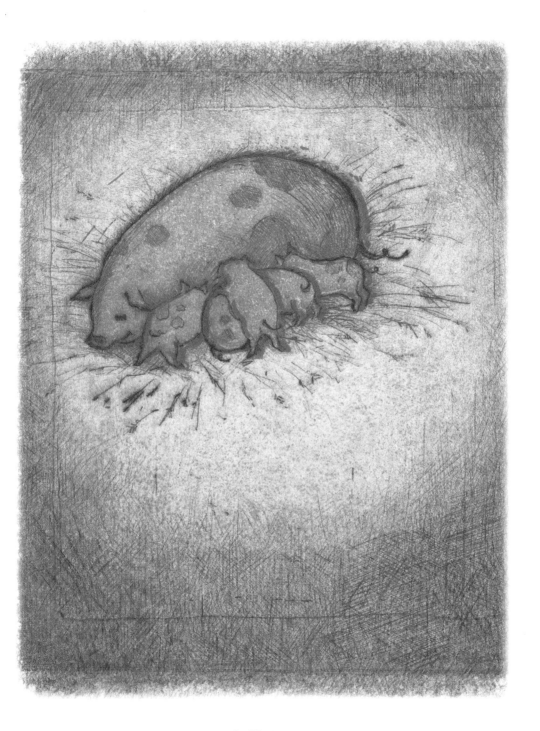

one pig, contentedly lying on his side in the dirt and the warm darkness, sleeping and dreaming, snoring with pleasure, snuffling and snorting.

Feeling a bit unnerved, I called the friend with the mother pig for reassurance. In fine detail, he related the story of watching an enormous boar being led around a show ring, somehow pulling loose from his chain, and in front of everyone, breaking off his owner's leg. True or not, this grisly, graphic tale had its effect. I began leaving the food pail at the top of the hillside, just inside the gate, when the pigs were off foraging. I now spoke with the pigs and scratched their backs only from outside the fence. From their point of view, my change in attitude must have been confusing. After all, most pig owners would have been pleased and proud of such stupendous-sized pigs. Instead, I was disappointingly wary and worried.

In the end, both pigs died suddenly and mysteriously, the very night before slaughtering. My early confidence had clearly been unfounded, my understanding of pigs part of a storybook realm. I never did think of these animals as future food. We compared them to Wilbur in *Charlotte's Web*, and even the one named Hamlet conjured up the image of a prince, rather than ham and eggs. Their death was a sad event. I was certain they died of broken hearts, feeling betrayed by my strange change of behavior. They could have suffered heart failure from overeating. We never did know. And we never did try to raise another pig.

⌁ RAISING BEES ⌁

We began raising bees knowing little about the subject and on a grander scale than was either sensible or necessary. This was the very same summer I tended a fifty-foot row of planted peanuts only to learn that peanuts do not mature in the far north.

Our bees, however, did surprisingly well because the season was unusually warm and bright. They worked about in the sunny hay-fields, busily collecting nectar, searching out clover, fireweed, and the many other pretty wildflowers scattered over the countryside.

During the last days of August, just before summer turned to fall, we decided to extract the honey. Following a neighbour's suggestion, we took the frames out of the hives when most of the bees were away collecting and vacuumed off those who had stayed behind; then we loaded the frames into the back of our truck and hurried home. We carried these frames, heavy and dripping with honey, into the kitchen. The extractor was set on the table, ready to go, but everything else was in a state of disarray. We had spent the morning slaughtering and plucking chickens for the first time, and as a result of our efforts, naked chickens lay cooling in the bathtub and feathers everywhere else.

With a warm knife, we removed the wax capping from the first two frames and set them into the extractor. The children began in turn to crank the handle, spinning out the golden honey. There was a most amazing amount of honey — delicious unpasteurized honey, which provided not only flowery sweetening but also the most medicinal balm known to man for the treatment of burns. We didn't have enough containers for it all. And, of course, with the filling of numerous jars, various buckets and bowls, and all available pots and pans, dribbles were dripped everywhere. The chicken feathers now became stuck in the spilled honey.

Optimistically, I continued tidying the kitchen, wiping up the excess honey and feathers with newspapers, crumpling them into

wads, and stuffing them into the wood stove. A few curious bees appeared at the windows to watch our antics. After a time they disappeared, but soon returned, bringing with them their many friends. We were now under siege, with hundreds and hundreds of angry bees darkening the windows.

The honey operation was definitely out of control. One could not blame the bees, for they had worked without cease all summer long. It is said that each pound of honey represents ten million foraging flights for gathering nectar, and we had suddenly and unfairly snatched away this food supply in a minute. The bees were justifiably indignant and intent on recovering their stolen goods. A great roar of buzzing began in the chimney when they discovered the honeyed newspapers and dove down to the rescue. Like a scene from a comic book, the stove nearly burst with the buzzing. Lighting a match to the sticky papers was impossible, for opening the stove door even a crack would have let loose a stream of angry bees.

Unbelievably, just then there was a knock on the door, as yet another unexpected visitor arrived on the scene. Thankfully, it was not a neighbour, but the mother-in-law of one of my husband's university colleagues, an opera singer who had earlier brought his young children for a stay. Now his mother-in-law from England was hoping for a country holiday.

How could this be happening? No longer just one scene, but now a whole comic strip unfolded before my eyes. The proper English lady looked in horror at the situation in our kitchen. Quickly and wisely she fled, never to be heard from again.

I felt like doing much the same. Instead, it was my husband who went on his way. The next morning he returned to his university job, leaving behind a house in disarray, hives of frustrated bees, and a long list of unfinished chores.

∿ FALL DAYS ∿

Without exception, our late summer days were jammed full of rush and confusion, reason enough to savour the restful quiet of fall. There were few visitors now; just the children and I did the chores and finished up the garden. As another growing season came to an end, we picked the remaining beans for freezing, made applesauce and chutney, pickled crabapples, and juiced heaps of carrots.

Shadows grew longer and days perceptibly shorter. Heavy rains fell, but most often a glorious Indian summer followed behind the first frost. Nights turned cold and clear, with myriads of sparkling stars sprinkled across the darkness and the Milky Way like an enchanted river lighting the heavens. Only the afternoons still held onto the sun's warmth, touched now with a soft and fragile stillness of the last butterflies. Time slowed, as the earth paused, gathering in the holy radiance of the changing seasons.

The valley, like a great golden bowl, filled with light and a thousand trees shining bright in the autumn sun. We should have all taken time to sit and stare, to breathe in this beauty, to store away the memory for rekindling on some dark and dreary day. But no one stopped, for there was always work to be done.

Meanwhile, gold rained down upon the hills like spattering paint, and the leaves, like blotting paper, absorbed the colour. Each single leaf turned from green to gold; each followed the pattern of its own kind. The daintily serrated leaves of the birch were edged with yellow, spreading inward like a magic stain. Accents of rich red, and sometimes dark purple, splashed onto the occasional vine or shrub dotted across the landscape.

But for all its splendour, this season was edged with melancholy. Signs of passing time and coming winter were everywhere evident. The spectacular show was short lived, a warm burst of colour before the cold and dark of winter. Leaves began to fall one by one. Then

gentle breezes changed to strong winds, blowing the leaves down in drifts, covering roots and land with golden brown. Trees stood empty and bare once again, beautiful branches shadowed on the frosty grass and silhouetted against an ashen grey sky. Fresh snow fell onto the mountaintops, gradually veiling the high country in lacy white. Soon the whole valley would turn to winter's white.

The change could be unmercifully abrupt. The ground could freeze without warning, one time forcing us to dig blocks of icy soil and carrots, load wheelbarrows with mittened hands, and run for the house, repeatedly dumping the contents into the back room, creating the strangest and messiest root cellar imaginable.

Brussels sprouts were a favoured vegetable in the valley simply because they required no such attention. One had only to venture out into the snow and hack off some sprouts when preparing for a meal. When snows were deep, no one had to eat Brussels sprouts anymore.

⤐ Falling into Place ⤏

Although there was still work to be done, the fall was not nearly as busy as the spring and summer. As the days closed in, we stopped our work and came inside earlier, allowing at least a bit of time for reflection, a quiet time most often late at night. I was aware then of the surrounding countryside as a backdrop of strong and quiet beauty. From our open hillside, surrounded by fields and woods, we overlooked the valley — a valley, created over centuries by its wide and winding river, now silver in the moonlight.

On the far side, evergreen forests grew up the mountains, reaching to the rocky peaks above. Light and shadow played across this landscape, continuously changing its colours and contours. Clouds gathered around the high peaks, frequently darkening the sky, sending thunder and rainstorms out across the valley. Many days, the late afternoon sun dropped below the charcoal-grey cloud cover, briefly illuminating the valley and the birches, setting them aglow like candles lighting the dark forest. Rainbows appeared as if by magic — double, sometimes even triple.

Seasons came and went in this valley, as they had since time unknown. Weather played about peaks that forever stretched away into the distance, great waves in an endless sea of mountains.

The farms below were mere dots on the land, and our particular farm problems insignificant. I was aware of being infinitely small in an immense universe of natural magnificence. This landscape, which was to me a first frightening, at last came to be greatly reassuring. The place which in the beginning seemed a far cry from home, in the end began to feel in some ways like home. Aside from the scars left by clear-cut logging, this was a place apart, somewhere man had not totally trampled and destroyed for his own resources. The very inhospitable nature of the landscape helped to preserve its rugged beauty.

⤞ Travelling with Turkeys ⤝

Unusual migrations were part of our life, and our northern neighbours must have found these forays back and forth both amusing and incomprehensible. We routinely crammed the car as full as possible, closed up the farmhouse for another season, and set off. We travelled over the same roads many times from Jasper to Banff, passing through magnificent mountain country — wild, high peaks and big, open valleys. Within this extraordinary setting, we made our way back and forth, like a tiny caravan of migrating gypsy bugs.

Our turkeys too were unusually well travelled, adding to the expense of raising them. The fluffy young were purchased in Calgary, along with their feed, and then chauffeured three hundred fifty miles north to our farm. We kept these newly hatched babies under constant watch — inside, protected from drafts, and warmed by a heat lamp. If frightened by any loud noise, such as a ringing telephone, the tiny birds would all dash to huddle together, so tightly bunched that one or two could easily suffocate. A few in their panic might fall into their water dish and drown.

Even grown turkeys are known to behave foolishly when alarmed. My neighbour told of a whole flock that frantically plunged one after another into a pond, frightened to death by the sound of an airplane passing in the area. We also had a large pond, but luckily seldom any aircraft overhead. There were other hazards, however — noisy farm equipment, the occasional blast of a shotgun, and frequent crashing thunder.

In spite of these disturbances, the turkeys grew quickly and were soon wandering about freely, helping themselves to the innumerable delicacies that a farmyard has to offer — juicy worms and caterpillars, tasty bugs and grubs, delicious green grasses, and delectable findings of spilled grain. Because they liked to roost up high, the turkeys were

usually safe from resident coyotes. Our flock favoured the garage roof, where they often gathered at dusk, lined up in their feathered finery, like sentries all in a row.

One fall, our family made the trip back to Calgary together, hauling the turkeys with us, another three hundred fifty miles for their final fattening. Neighbour children were drawn, as to a country fair, to watch our unusual preparations and departure. In a flurry of activity and confusion, we piled the truck high with an odd assortment of belongings — the usual grain sacks of fresh vegetables and crates of canned fruit, but also gear for every imaginable sport — canoeing, cycling, climbing, skiing, and even fencing. Although we had barely a spare minute for any recreation, we still continued to haul this unused equipment around for years, packing and unpacking it.

With the children and my dog as travelling companions, I drove along behind the truck. We watched the crates of nearly grown turkeys balanced awkwardly on either side of the load and an upside down tricycle, tied on top of a pile of sheepskins — the crowning touch. Its pedals, caught by the wind, engaged the front wheel, setting it turning, squeaking like a strange spinning pinwheel.

The turkeys, a bit dim but ever curious, stuck their heads out of the crates, stretching and bending their necks, feathers ruffled and wattles blowing in the wind, craning to take in this wondrous sight. They gawked in dismay — as did any passersby.

Not for the first time, we seemed more like a troop of travelling jesters than serious farmers. Certainly none of our neighbours moved livestock from place to place in such a manner.

When at last we arrived at our city home, neighbourhood children there also gathered to watch, this time as turkeys were unloaded, freed from their crates and herded into an enclosed pen. Our boys delighted in dumping buckets of crabapples into this pen, littering the ground, making it difficult for the turkeys to move about. Like clumsy, red-headed clowns, the turkeys struggled to keep upright on the rolling apples, performing a balancing act, tottering and wobbling unsteadily.

At last gaining a foothold, they stood stupidly gazing at the apples. With lowered heads and swaying rubber-like necks, they cast about, until suddenly one would snatch up a tasty crabapple, lift its head high, and, as a heron catching a fish, swallow its prize down whole. The other turkeys watched with interest, the children cheered as the tiny apple slid down the turkey's throat like a falling Adam's apple, and I was grateful that someone besides me was for the moment providing a bit of comic relief.

◡ᵂ WINTER WARMING ᵂ◠

Our house construction, like our first northern migration, began with surprisingly little in the way of planning — a few stakes in the ground and a few huge abandoned bridge timbers started us off on the project. At this time, good lumber was plentiful and inexpensive, so we built a California type house, cedar-shaked, with high ceilings and large windows. The old house was conveniently connected to the new by an outside walkway leading also to the laundry and shower rooms. It was a fine summer arrangement, but by fall, the walkway, the farm and the mountains were all enshrouded in clouds of mist and pouring rain. When the weather cleared, the nights turned frosty and suddenly very cold.

By this time, my husband was back at the university, often expounding to eager young students upon the benefits of country living.

It was late September when the new water pipes froze. Talking with my neighbour, learning what to do, and finding equipment to do it, took most of the morning. Fortunately, the pipes were located under the outside walkway, ensuring handy access for the blowtorch. Unfortunately, the resulting water flow lasted only until nightfall, when once again the temperature plummeted like a sinking stone.

A small wood stove for cooking warmed the old house, along with a big wood heater located in the cellar, at the bottom of dangerously steep cement stairs. As an afterthought we had also installed a medium sized wood stove in the new house. My job — between caring for the farm, the animals and the children — was to keep these hearth fires burning, with just the right amount and the right kind of wood. I collected kindling continuously, for my fires tended to be temperamental and in frequent need of rekindling, frustrating when I remembered my rooftop fire, blazing away, burning steadily, and stubbornly refusing to be extinguished.

For my neighbours, the cold weather brought a bit of rest, but for me it brought new challenges. My first attempts at wood splitting

were exasperating and downright dangerous. The wood refused to stay balanced for the attack, and when the ax did connect, it jammed itself inconsiderately into the wood. To make matters worse, as often happened during troubling times, the neighbours appeared to watch. My efforts succeeded in causing concern as well as providing entertainment, even when I improved enough to begin splitting what seemed a great pile of wood.

Did I know that wood should be split a year in advance for proper seasoning? Did I know how much wood I might need for a northern winter? Probably ten cords for our unusually designed house. To me, this was the equivalent of ten small sized mountains. Did I want to buy some wood? Indeed I did. These truckloads had only to be stacked, piled and carried to the appropriate heaters.

That first winter, however, I did not really know if the house was properly warmed. I was mostly outside, busy with chores, frozen pipes, and collecting kindling.

⊰ BEELINE FOR VICTORIA ⊱

For many years, I was away from the farm only during the winter months. This migration pattern changed when we bought a home in Victoria, and the children at last began attending school regularly. Now we returned to the farm just for the summer months, thereby condensing the workload even more, turning the season into nothing but a non-stop rush of chores. By the end of August, we were swallowed up in a frenzied flurry of activity, and at the same time had to prepare once again for a major move southward.

We spent most of the night packing. First we loaded a big freezer into the van and filled it with frozen meat and berries, then we packed in boxes of canned goods, sacks of carrots, potatoes, onions, and squashes, gear of every description and paraphernalia of every kind, and last we loaded the beehives, under cover of darkness, with the swarms of occupants at rest, their entranceways sealed shut to close off all means of escape.

The car also was crammed full. As well as four children (one rode with my husband in the van) and the dog, I carried clothing of all kinds, a half-size cello, varied books and papers, my sewing machine and associated materials, plus everyone's summer treasures — bug collections, favourite feathers, pressed flowers, and assorted summer projects of every description.

We headed off early in the morning, not the least bit rested, with five hundred miles of highway before us. At the last moment, a kind-hearted neighbour girl appeared bearing gifts of potted aloe plants and a whipped cream cheese cake, sadly destined to slide off its plate within the first few miles. It is astonishing that this departure seemed quite ordinary to me at the time. The major concern was that we reach our destination before the last ferry crossing. The prospect of spending a night parked on the dock with our beehives and several hundred pounds of thawing meat was incentive enough to speed us

along our way (carrying somewhere extra extension cords for just such an emergency).

Our trip was relatively uneventful for about two hundred miles. Then one of the children noticed a few bees inside the back window of the van. We all watched as more and more bees appeared, one by one darkening the window, like the slow motion return of a bad dream. Resourceful and ready to enter into the spirit of the moment, the children found pen and paper, drew a big bee, labeled "B", and held it up to the window as I zoomed up next to the van.

Our small procession slowed to a stop, and we all piled out to assess the situation. We discovered that one of the hives had been jostled apart, probably as we travelled over the rough and rutted road leading away from our farm. Seeing a crack of light, the worker bees decided it was time for collecting nectar, and were both anxious and determined to carry out this appointed task. Bees are devoted to their work and dislike any disruption in routine. This peculiar day on the move was definitely not to their liking.

We hung a blanket behind the front seat, hoping in vain the bees would remain content to crawl over the back window. But why would they want to watch the grassy roadsides and sweet wildflowers from inside the window? Humming with excitement, they were frantic to get out, flying towards any tiny glimmer of light and exiting from every small rusted hole they could find. A steady steam issued forth like a fountain from an old crack near the exhaust pipe. We stuffed in a piece of rag and hastily continued on our way, for as long as we kept moving, the bees did not dare venture forth.

Stopping only briefly for gas, we sped along the open, empty highway, arriving at the ferry unexpectedly early, before dark. The flaw in our timing was immediately apparent, as the frustrated bees began flying off again, one by one. Nearby travellers watched uneasily, climbed back into their vehicles and rolled up their windows. My husband and older son walked about nonchalantly, stuffing toilet paper into the offending rust holes.

In the car, I pretended not to notice and tried to concentrate on reading a book. The minutes ticked slowly by until time for loading.

Then I felt as if we were sneaking on board with hidden explosives. Any anxious traveller had every right to report us, and any ferry worker had good reason to stop us — but no one did.

We drove on board without incident and eased into our parking places. The whine of the ship's engines disguised the agitated hum of our unhappy hives, but just one glance at our van, and nearby passengers quickly headed for the stairs, deserting the car deck. We searched for a discarded newspaper and taped it over the back window to hide the buzzing bees from sight. After that, there seemed nothing more to do but head upstairs ourselves to the buffet dinner. This unusual treat was not a restful meal, however, for I kept imagining bombarding bees chasing unhappy passengers, and expected any minute to be summoned over the intercom.

When our ferry finally neared the terminal, we returned to the car deck with apprehension. Amazingly, all was quiet. Not a bee was stirring. Not even one bee was in sight. Inadvertently, we had found the solution to our problem. Covering the windows had brought about sudden nightfall within the van, encouraging the bees to retreat into their hive to rest in spite of the burning lights brightening the car deck. This was an unexpected turn of events and a happy ending to our journey.

Of course, had we understood more about bees, we would not have had such a problem to begin with and certainly would not have hit upon the solution by happenstance. (Soon after our trip, the ferries began requiring hives to be sealed shut and strapped together, thereby avoiding any such mishap.)

It was nearing midnight when we arrived home. Now we had only to unload the bees and plug in the freezer, and then we could sleep. School would begin, and I would again be mostly on my own with the children and our dog. But we were in a beautiful place, close to the ocean, with mild days ahead, no farm chores and no predators. For me, the end of summer signaled the beginning of my rest time.

By now I did question the benefits and reasons for farming in this way. Living in two places, with five children, necessarily involved a great deal of packing and unpacking. My husband had certainly not learned the lesson of simplicity from the nomadic peoples he so admired. We were burdened down with belongings, and inevitably some of these — canning jars, wooden spoons, pairs of scissors, unmatched socks, or special tools — were left behind at the wrong house.

To add to these complications, my husband made other trips to other lands between our farm migrations. The family had to adapt, continually making ready for either coming or going, with not enough time to appreciate where we were or concentrate on what we were doing.

We carried on moving back and forth to the farm a few more times, until the whole operation made absolutely no sense whatsoever. My energy for this unsettled life was at last spent.

⌒ TURNING TO THE PRESENT ⌒

With some troubles and trials, the rewards are seen only from a distance, perhaps looking back at the past. So it was with our farming adventure. My days far away on the farm were seasons of learning, unknown to me at the time, only to be understood many years later. First of all, I learned how to work, mostly by trying to follow the example of my Mennonite neighbours. Soon I came to love working, enjoying the very tangible rewards of my labour — a growing garden, properly cared for; canning jars filled, their colours lining the shelves; wood neatly stacked, ready for winter.

My children also learned to work hard. Trying their best in sometimes difficult situations, they became a strong and supportive team. They had the good fortune also to play in the fields and the barn, to care for animals, newly born and fully grown, and to be at home in the natural world, perhaps to hear the secret sounds of its beauty.

Nature was not just a piece of this life, rather it filled our days. We were a part of our surroundings, like the ever-present, but tiny figures in a Chinese painting, and blessed to have everyday experiences connected to the land. My own child-life had been happily spent mostly out-of-doors. Today's children often do not feel so at ease in the world of nature, and if they feel no kinship with the earth, how will they be comforted by their landscape? Computers are no substitute for being friendly with a special tree. Feeling no kinship with the land, how will these children possibly learn to respect and care for this our only earth-home and its precious natural resources?

⌒

I remember my two little daughters snuggled into bed one night, between them a small bird resting on a doll-sized pillow, his head tucked under his wing, a wing broken and gently bandaged with a tiny splint. I remember too the children excitedly gathered around in the growing darkness, watching in awe the miracle of a luna moth

drawn to the light of our window. We were fortunate to have no television. Instead we had real experiences; we made things and told stories.

One summer we studied a beautiful birch clump, systematically counting and collecting bugs, observing bird life, making little drawings, collecting seeds and leaves, and taking notes several times a day, every day, in every weather. Thinking back on this experience, I am certain that becoming friendly with a birch clump is one of the more optimistic and reassuring of life's lessons. For me it must have been so, for I dreamt of being buried beneath this tree, nestled among its roots, feeling totally at peace. Such dreams of the spirit are surely encouraged by living close to the land. This land, so taken for granted, is valuable beyond price and beyond any reckoning. It is the very center of nature's intricate web, supporting all of life.

Over the years, I slowly came to recognize and appreciate the splendour and enormous beauty of my rugged landscape. I breathed in my surroundings, gradually soaking up the scents and images about me, until somehow this world took hold of my heart and crept into my soul. Our little farm, plotted and pieced together, situated in this beautiful valley, grew dear to me. The country which at first seemed a far cry from home, at last began to feel like home, at least for the part of the year when it was not buried in snow and ice. I felt tied to the earth and to its plants and trees, a connection which is now part of my being, a sensitivity that allows me to feel alive and in tune with my world.

I can still see clumps of lady slippers in tall grasses and tiny, delicate wildflowers hidden deep in the darkness of mossy woods. In the springtime, delicious and exotic mushrooms pushed their way up through moist earth and decaying leaves. We searched for morels, as for buried treasure, and came home with basketsful, God's blessing to observant winter survivors.

I can see also the huge cottonwood living in our pasture, its high branches outstretched, its summer seeds floating down in a cloudburst of fluff, piling up softly on our porch steps. The birch seeds fell later in the season, pattering down like fine rain, providing a feast for gathering birds. Magically the trees filled with little striped pine siskins, happily pecking at the ripened seed cones.

In summer frequent refreshing rains stirred the sweet scent of wet fields and fresh-cut hay. Changing clouds moved continuously about the mountain peaks and across the valley. Leaves fell and the moon rested in the empty branches of the birch tree. Snow sifted down over the valley and piled in deep drifts, shadowed by the lovely, ancient patterns of bare branches and trees bathed in moonlight.

But in spite of this great natural beauty, if I had stayed on our farm, I would have been by now physically worn out. In spite of the strength and reassurance in those timeless mountains, I had to leave the valley. Endless hard work can cause almost anyone sometimes to despair, and I was never suited to this extreme situation.

At an early age, I had imagined myself as an artist. When I married, I naively assumed this pattern would continue, simply because it was important to me. Instead, my life followed a different pattern. Repetitious physical labour became a way of life. Perhaps because I was young, this new experience was at first interesting and challenging.

My housekeeping required setting a veritable trap line for mice, continually filling woodbins and carrying out ashes from the wood-stoves. Preparing food included not only cooking and baking, but weeding, harvesting, canning and freezing. Caring for my children involved home schooling. Sewing included making clothes, knitting sweaters, and also mending and patching of all kinds, both inside and outside of the house, a brave attempt to somehow hold the pieces together.

These were not tasks I ever saw performed by my mother, nor was I schooled in such practices. But in spite of these drawbacks, there were rewards, and one of the most important was having children working together. There was, however, almost always too much work, and at times I wanted to cry from tiredness, seeing all that needed to be done, and remembering more gentle surroundings and a softer climate. I often worked late into the night, sometimes until I was too tired to even stand. Feeling sorry for myself was not helpful. After all, my neighbours worked much harder than I. And, as my husband liked to point out, there were places in the world where women had none of my advantages.

৵

Now many years have passed, years of happy, productive times mixed with difficulties, disappointments, and different responsibilities. For all that, to my astonishment and satisfaction, I find myself today following my own path and living a life of my own choosing.

I live in a beautiful part of the world, surrounded by an ever-changing sea and small rocky islands. I have an acre of land to garden, room to create my own small and peaceful world, and time to give attention to this work. This landscape is different from the north; its very hospitable nature is its own disadvantage. Not far away and crowding ever closer, are signs of growing population — destruction of trees and farmland, disappearing nature, and pollution of earth and water. The speed of change is frightening.

This loss is all the more reason to pay heed to that which remains; the destruction reason enough for creating something else of beauty. It is, after all, still a beautiful world, if only we can learn to see, to keep faith in the earth's goodness, and to watch for that mystic night when the moon will light the rainbow.

Attempting to record the secret sounds of beauty, I engage in a work close to my heart. This is a pleasure I once considered commonplace and now recognize as a profound privilege.

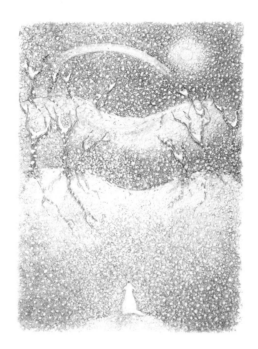

These illustrations (like those in Helen's book A Child's Enchanted Garden)
are reproduced from original intaglio prints.

The images are handprinted by the artist,
using multiple handworked copper plates.

The unique qualities of traditional printmaking techniques
(including drypoint, aquatint, soft ground, flat bite and spit bite)
result in beautifully layered and richly textured images.

"Consider the gentle creatures of the earth
And grant their innocence may touch mankind"